Experiment with What a Plant Needs to Grow

Nadia Higgins

Lerner Publications
Minneapolis

Lerner Publications Company
A division of Lerner Publishing Group, Inc.
241 First Avenue North
Minneapolis, MN 55401 USA

For reading levels and more information, look up this title at www.lernerbooks.com.

Library of Congress Cataloging-in-Publication Data

Higgins, Nadia.
    Experiment with what a plant needs to grow / by Nadia Higgins.
        pages cm. — (Lightning bolt books™ — Plant experiments)
    Includes index.
    ISBN 978-1-4677-5730-0 (lib. bdg. : alk. paper)
    ISBN 978-1-4677-6247-2 (eBook)
    1. Growth (Plants)—Juvenile literature. 2. Plants—Experiments—Juvenile literature. I. Title.
  II. Series: Lightning bolt books. Plant experiments.
    QK745.H54 2015
    571.8'2—dc23   2014020465

Manufactured in the United States of America
1 — BP — 12/31/14

Table of Contents

What Will a Plant Do to Find Light?

Plants are living things. They grow. They reproduce. Like you, plants need air and water. They need minerals to stay healthy. They also need food.

With enough sunlight and water, flowering plants will bloom.

For a plant, food starts with sunlight. Sunlight fuels photosynthesis. This is a process in which green leaves make food using air and water.

Plants give us food, wood, and medicine. Photosynthesis provides the oxygen we need to breathe!

Let's take a look at what plants will do to get life-giving light.

What you need:

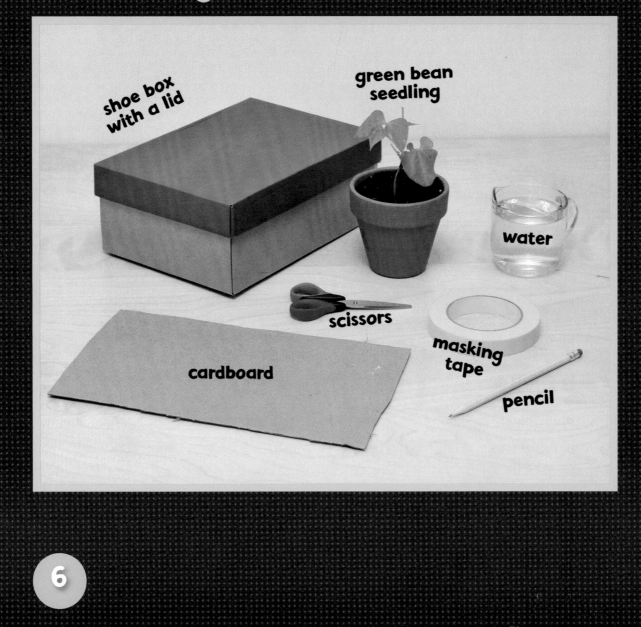

shoe box with a lid

green bean seedling

water

scissors

cardboard

masking tape

pencil

Steps:

1. Cut a window on one end of the box.

2. Place the other end of the box on top of the cardboard. Trace around the end of the box so you are drawing a rectangle. Have an adult help you cut out the rectangle. Then cut it in half.

The window should take up about one-third of the end of the box.

Space out your cardboard pieces like this.

3. Tape the cardboard pieces inside the shoe box, like shelves, leaving enough room to place your potted seedling inside the box.

4. Set the box upright so that the window is on top. Place the seedling under the shelves. Next, put on the lid.

Keep your box in a sunny spot. Take off the lid to water it every few days.

Think It Through

What happens to your plant as it grows? It bends through the cardboard maze you created. Why does it do this? To find the light!

The bean plant can tell where the sunlight is. It grows toward the light it needs.

Does Fertilizer Help Marigolds Grow?

Most plants grow in soil. Soil holds the water plants need to grow. Soil also provides minerals, such as iron and calcium.

You need calcium, just as plants do. You can get this mineral from milk and other foods.

Minerals are like vitamins for plants. They keep plants healthy. Let's grow marigolds in two kinds of soil. One pot has soil with fertilizer, which adds minerals. One does not.

Roots help a plant take in minerals from the soil.

Will the minerals make a difference in how tall the plant grows? Let's find out!

What you need:

two marigold seedlings

two pots the same size

organic fertilizer

shovel

plain potting soil

water

pencil and paper

Popsicle stick

ruler

Make sure your marigold seedlings are close to the same size.

Steps:

1. Fill both pots with potting soil.

2. With an adult's help, add fertilizer to just one of the pots. The directions on the package will tell you how much to add.

Put a Popsicle stick in the fertilizer pot so you can remember which one it is.

Next, it's time for planting!

3. Dig a hole in each pot.

4. Remove the marigold seedlings from their containers and plant them in the holes.

The holes should be the same size as the marigolds' roots.

Check your plants every day and add water if the soil is dry.

5. Fill in the holes with soil and gently press down. Water each pot well.

6. Put the pots in a sunny window. Add water to keep the soil from drying out.

After a few days, you'll see your plants get taller.

7. Measure your plants' heights once a week for three weeks.

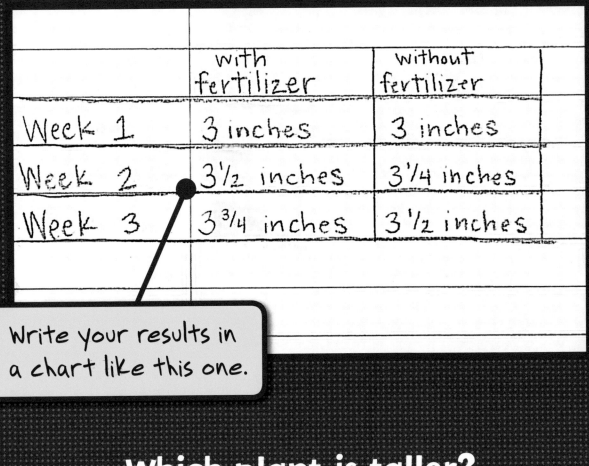

	with fertilizer	without fertilizer	
Week 1	3 inches	3 inches	
Week 2	3½ inches	3¼ inches	
Week 3	3¾ inches	3½ inches	

Write your results in a chart like this one.

Which plant is taller?

Some gardeners add fertilizer to their plants to add more minerals to the soil.

Think It Through

Water, sunshine, and air made both plants grow. But minerals gave one of them a boost. The taller marigold took in needed minerals from the fertilizer. Did you notice any other differences between the two plants?

Can Seeds Get Too Much Water?

Water helps a plant stay strong and sturdy. But even before a plant shoots out of the ground, its seeds need water to sprout.

Plants die if they don't get enough water.

Can seeds get too much water? Let's find out.

What you need:

water

three small bowls

handful of grass seeds

six cotton balls

pencil and paper

Steps:

1. Start by putting two cotton balls in each of the bowls.

2. Next, fill the first bowl so the cotton balls are covered with water. Moisten the second bowl's cotton balls all the way through. Don't add any water to the third bowl.

3. Sprinkle about a dozen seeds on top of the cotton balls in each bowl.

Very Wet

A little Wet

Dry

Label the bowls so you remember which is which.

4. Put the cotton balls in a sunny place.

5. Check the bowls every day. Make sure the first two cotton balls stay covered in water. Make sure the second two stay moist.

After a few days, some seeds will sprout.

Very Wet

A little Wet

Dry

Keep checking your seedlings for a week. Which sprouts are the tallest and sturdiest?

Horse chestnuts have spiky seed coats to protect their seeds.

Think It Through

A seed has a coat that protects it. Water softens the coat, so the seed can sprout. But seeds also need air. Too much water can keep a seed from getting enough air.

Now Try This

Earlier in the book, you learned that plants need minerals to be healthy. Most plants get minerals from the soil. Predict how long your grass can survive without soil. Watch the grass sprouts to see if you were right.

Be sure to write down your prediction before you start experimenting.

How Do Leaves Get Air?

We just saw that seeds need air to sprout. Roots need air too. Air is also part of photosynthesis.

You can easily poke your finger into good garden soil. The loose soil holds lots of tiny spaces. Those air-filled spaces keep roots healthy.

As they make food, green leaves take air in and let it out. Let's find out how.

What you need:

petroleum jelly

leafy green plant

masking tape

camera

Steps:

1. Spread a heavy coat of petroleum jelly over the tops of five leaves of your plant.

2. Do the same on the undersides of five other leaves.

3. Put your plant in a sunny window. Then take its picture.

4. Observe your plant every day for the next week.

Mark the tops of the coated leaves with tape so you can easily find them again.

Compare what you see to the photo you took on the first day.

How are the leaves different from your photo?

Think It Through
Petroleum jelly kept some of the leaves from letting air in and out. Those leaves started to wilt. The leaves that were coated on the bottom wilted the most.

Measure Like a Scientist

Measuring helps scientists show exactly what is happening. Let's look at some ways you might use measuring in a plant experiment.

Measurement	Test	Tool	Unit (metric)
Weight	Weigh two seeds. Is one heavier?	Scale	Ounces (grams)
Length	Measure a bean seedling in the morning. Then measure it the next day. Did it grow taller?	Ruler	Inches (centimeters)
Time	Track how many days it takes for a plant to bloom.	Calendar	Days
Volume	Measure how much water you are adding to a pot.	Measuring cup	Cup (milliliters)

Fun Facts

- Your body is about six-tenths water. A plant is about nine-tenths water.

- Why don't seeds sprout inside fruit? After all, fruits are moist. They provide seeds with water. It's because most fruits have substances that keep the seeds from sprouting.

- A Venus flytrap grows in soil that has few minerals. The plant feasts on insects to get the minerals it needs. Its leaves clamp together, trapping bugs inside. Then plant juices digest the bugs' soft insides.

- A large tree can take in 100 gallons (380 liters) of water in a single day. That's the same amount as one hundred jugs of milk!

Glossary

fertilizer: a substance that gardeners add to soil to make it rich in minerals

mineral: a substance that living things need to stay healthy

observe: to notice like a scientist

photosynthesis: the process green plants use to make food using sunlight, water, and air

predict: to make a good guess about what might happen in the future

reproduce: to make babies, young animals, or new plants

root: a plant part that takes in water and minerals

seedling: a young plant

Further Reading

Easy Science for Kids: Plants
http://easyscienceforkids.com/plants

Glaser, Linda. *Garbage Helps Our Garden Grow: A Compost Story.* Minneapolis: Millbrook Press, 2010.

Mullins, Matt. *Think Like a Scientist in the Garden.* Ann Arbor, MI: Cherry Lake, 2012.

National Gardening Association: Kids Gardening
http://www.kidsgardening.org

Sterling, Kristin. *Exploring Seeds.* Minneapolis: Lerner Publications, 2012.

University of Illinois Extension:
The Great Plant Escape
http://urbanext.illinois.edu/gpe/index.cfm

Index

Photo Acknowledgments

The images in this book are used with the permission of: © Rick Orndorf, pp. 2, 6, 7, 8, 9, 12, 13, 14, 15, 19, 20, 21, 25, 26, 27; © Lucian Coman/Shutterstock Images, p. 4; © Koichi Saito/a.collectionRF/Thinkstock, p. 5; © Jupiterimages/Thinkstock, pp. 10, 22, 23; © Richard Griffin/Shutterstock Images, p. 11; © Red Line Editorial, p. 16; © Katarzyna Bialasiewicz/Thinkstock, p. 17; © Ansis Klucis/Shutterstock Images, p. 18; © monkeybusinessimages/Thinkstock, p. 24; © sergeyskleznev/Thinkstock, p. 30; © Seiya Kawamoto/Thinkstock, p. 31.

Front cover: © Rick Orndorf

Main body text set in Johann Light 30/36.